salad
days

MURDOCH
B O O K S

Fattoush

2 pitta bread rounds (17 cm/
   6¾ inch diameter)
6 cos (romaine) lettuce leaves,
   shredded
1 large Lebanese (short) cucumber,
   cubed
4 tomatoes, cut into 1 cm (½ inch)
   cubes
8 spring onions (scallions), chopped
4 tablespoons finely chopped flat-leaf
   (Italian) parsley
1 tablespoon finely chopped mint
2 tablespoons finely chopped
   coriander (cilantro)

Dressing
2 garlic cloves, crushed
100 ml (3½ fl oz) extra virgin olive oil
100 ml (3½ fl oz) lemon juice

Preheat the oven to moderate 180°C
(350°F/Gas 4). Split the bread in half
through the centre and bake on
a baking tray for 8–10 minutes,
or until golden and crisp, turning
halfway through. Break into pieces.

To make the dressing, whisk all the
ingredients together in a bowl until
well combined.

Place the bread and remaining salad
ingredients in a serving bowl and toss
to combine. Drizzle with the dressing
and toss well. Season to taste with
salt and freshly ground black pepper.
Serve immediately.

Serves 6

Note: This is a popular Middle
Eastern peasant salad which
is served as an appetiser or
to accompany a light meal.

Prawn and bean salad

200 g (1 cup) dried cannellini beans
2 red capsicums (peppers), cut into
   large flattish pieces
300 g (10½ oz) green beans, trimmed
150 g (½ loaf) day-old ciabatta bread
   or other crusty loaf
80 ml (⅓ cup) olive oil
1 large garlic clove, finely chopped
1 kg (2 lb 4 oz) raw medium prawns
   (shrimp), peeled and deveined,
   with tails intact
30 g (1½ cups) flat-leaf (Italian)
   parsley

Dressing
60 ml (¼ cup) lemon juice
60 ml (¼ cup) olive oil
2 tablespoons capers, rinsed,
   drained and chopped
1 teaspoon sugar, optional

Soak the cannellini beans in a large
bowl of cold water for 8 hours. Drain
then rinse the beans well, transfer to
a saucepan, cover with cold water
and cook for 20–30 minutes, or until
tender. Drain, rinse under cold water,
drain again and put in a serving bowl.

Cook the capsicum, skin-side-up,
under a hot griller (broiler) until the
skin blackens and blisters. Cool in
a plastic bag, then peel. Cut into
strips, and add to the bowl.

Cook the green beans in a saucepan
of boiling water for 3–4 minutes, or
until tender. Drain and add to the
serving bowl. Cut the bread into six
slices, then cut each slice in four.
Heat 60 ml (¼ cup) of the oil in a
frying pan and cook the bread over
medium heat on each side until
golden. Remove from the pan.

Heat the remaining oil in the frying
pan, add the garlic and prawns and
cook for 1–2 minutes, or until the
prawns are pink and cooked. Add
to the salad with the parsley.

Combine the dressing ingredients,
then season. Toss the dressing and
bread through the salad.

Serves 4

Minced pork and noodle salad

1 tablespoon peanut oil
500 g (1 lb 2 oz) minced
  (ground) pork
2 garlic cloves, finely chopped
1 stalk lemon grass, finely chopped
2–3 red Asian shallots, thinly sliced
3 teaspoons finely grated fresh ginger
1 small red chilli, finely chopped
5 makrut (kaffir) lime leaves, very finely
  shredded
170 g (6 oz) glass (mung bean)
  noodles
60 g (2¼ oz) baby English spinach
  leaves
50 g (1 cup) roughly chopped
  coriander (cilantro)
170 g (6 oz) peeled, finely chopped
  fresh pineapple
10 g (½ cup) mint leaves

Dressing
1½ tablespoons shaved palm sugar
  or soft brown sugar
2 tablespoons fish sauce
80 ml (⅓ cup) lime juice
2 teaspoons sesame oil
2 teaspoons peanut oil, extra

Heat a wok until very hot, add the peanut oil and swirl to coat the wok. Add the pork and stir-fry in batches over high heat for 5 minutes, or until lightly golden. Add the garlic, lemon grass, shallots, grated ginger, chilli and lime leaves, and stir-fry for a further 1–2 minutes, or until fragrant.

Place the noodles in a large bowl and cover with boiling water for 30 seconds, or until softened. Rinse under cold water and drain well. Toss in a bowl with the spinach, coriander, pineapple, mint and pork mixture.

To make the dressing, mix together the palm sugar, fish sauce and lime juice. Add the sesame oil and extra peanut oil, and whisk to combine. Toss through the salad and season with freshly ground black pepper.

Serves 4

Artichoke, prosciutto and rocket salad

4 artichokes
2 eggs, lightly beaten
20 g (¼ cup) fresh breadcrumbs
25 g (¼ cup) grated Parmesan
  cheese
olive oil for frying, plus 1 tablespoon
  extra
8 slices prosciutto
3 teaspoons white wine vinegar
1 garlic clove, crushed
150 g (5½ oz) rocket (arugula), long
  stalks trimmed

shaved Parmesan cheese, optional
sea salt

Bring a large saucepan of water to the boil. Remove the hard outer leaves of each artichoke, trim the stem and cut 2–3 cm (¾–1¼ inches) off the top. Cut into quarters and remove the furry 'choke'. Boil the pieces for 2 minutes, then drain.

Whisk the eggs in a bowl and combine the seasoned breadcrumbs and grated Parmesan in another bowl. Dip each artichoke quarter into the egg, then roll in the crumb mixture to coat. Fill a frying pan with olive oil to a depth of 2 cm (¾ inch) and heat over medium–high heat. Add the artichokes in batches and fry for 2–3 minutes, or until golden. Remove from the pan and drain on paper towels.

Heat 1 tablespoon of olive oil in a non-stick frying pan over medium–high heat. Cook the prosciutto in two batches for 2 minutes, or until crisp and golden. Remove from the pan, reserving the oil.

Combine the reserved oil, vinegar and garlic with a little salt and pepper. Place the rocket in a bowl, add half of the salad dressing and toss well. Divide the rocket, artichokes and prosciutto among four plates, and drizzle with the remaining dressing. Garnish with shaved Parmesan, if desired, and sprinkle with sea salt.

Serves 4

Fusilli salad with sherry vinaigrette

300 g (10½ oz) fusilli
250 g (2 cups) cauliflower florets
125 ml (½ cup) olive oil
16 slices pancetta
10 g (½ cup) small sage leaves
100 g (⅔ cup) pine nuts, toasted
2 tablespoons finely chopped red
  Asian shallots
1½ tablespoons sherry vinegar
1 small red chilli, finely chopped
2 garlic cloves, crushed
1 teaspoon soft brown sugar
2 tablespoons orange juice
15 g (¾ cup) parsley, finely chopped
35 g (⅓ cup) shaved Parmesan
  cheese

Cook the fusilli in a large saucepan of rapidly boiling, salted water for 12 minutes, or until *al dente*. Drain and refresh under cold water until it is cool. Drain well. Blanch the cauliflower florets in boiling water for 3 minutes, then drain and cool.

Heat 1 tablespoon of olive oil in a non-stick frying pan and cook the pancetta for 2 minutes, or until crisp. Drain on crumpled paper towels. Add 1 more tablespoon of oil and cook the sage leaves for 1 minute, or until crisp. Drain on crumpled paper towels. In a large serving bowl, combine the pasta, pine nuts and cauliflower.

Heat the remaining olive oil, add the shallots and cook gently for 2 minutes, or until soft. Remove from the heat then add the vinegar, chilli, garlic, brown sugar, orange juice and chopped parsley. Pour the warm dressing over the pasta and toss gently to combine.

Place the salad in a serving bowl. Crumble the pancetta over the top and scatter with sage leaves and shaved Parmesan. Serve warm.

Serves 6

Squid salad with salsa verde

800 g (1 lb 12 oz) small–medium
  squid, cleaned, scored and sliced
  into 4 cm (1 1/2 inch) diamonds
2 tablespoons olive oil
2 tablespoons lime juice
150 g (5 1/2 oz) green beans
150 g (5 1/2 oz) asparagus spears
1 teaspoon olive oil, extra
100 g (3 1/2 oz) baby rocket (arugula)

Salsa verde
1 thick slice white bread, crusts
  removed
140 ml (5 fl oz) olive oil
3 tablespoons finely chopped parsley
2 teaspoons finely grated lemon zest
60 ml (1/4 cup) lemon juice
2 anchovy fillets, finely chopped
2 tablespoons capers, rinsed and
  drained
1 garlic clove, crushed

Combine the squid pieces in a bowl
with the olive oil, lime juice, and a
little salt and pepper, then cover
with plastic wrap and place in the
refrigerator to marinate for 2 hours.

To make the salsa verde, break the
bread into chunks and drizzle with
2 tablespoons of oil, mixing with your
hands so that the oil is absorbed.
Place the bread and remaining oil in
a food processor with the remaining
salsa ingredients, and blend to a
paste. If it is too thick, thin with lemon
juice and olive oil, to taste.

Trim the green beans and asparagus,
and cut in half on the diagonal.
Blanch the beans for 3 minutes,
refresh under cold water, then drain.
Blanch the asparagus for 1–2 minutes,
refresh in cold water, then drain.

Heat the extra oil in a frying pan over
high heat, and cook the marinated
squid in batches for 3 minutes per
batch, or until cooked. Cool slightly.

Combine the green beans,
asparagus, rocket and squid. Add
3 tablespoons of the salsa verde
and toss gently. Arrange on a serving
platter and drizzle with another
tablespoon of salsa verde.

Serves 4

Warm minted chicken and pasta salad

250 g (9 oz) cotelli pasta
125 ml ($\frac{1}{2}$ cup) olive oil
1 large red capsicum (pepper)
3 chicken breast fillets
6 spring onions (scallions), cut into
  2 cm ($\frac{3}{4}$ inch) lengths
4 garlic cloves, thinly sliced
35 g ($\frac{3}{4}$ cup) chopped mint
80 ml ($\frac{1}{3}$ cup) cider vinegar
100 g ($3\frac{1}{2}$ oz) baby English
  spinach leaves

Cook the pasta in a large saucepan of boiling water until *al dente*, drain, stir in 1 tablespoon of the oil and set aside. Meanwhile, cut the capsicum into quarters, removing the seeds and membrane. Place, skin-side-up, under a hot grill (broiler) for 8–10 minutes, or until the skin blackens and blisters. Cool in a plastic bag, then peel away the skin. Cut into thin strips. Place the chicken between two sheets of plastic wrap and press with the palm of your hand until slightly flattened.

Heat 1 tablespoon of the oil in a large frying pan, add the chicken and cook over medium heat for 2–3 minutes each side, or until light brown and cooked through. Remove from the pan and cut into 5 mm ($\frac{1}{4}$ inch) slices.

Add another tablespoon of the oil to the pan and add the spring onion, sliced garlic and capsicum and cook, stirring, for 2–3 minutes, or until starting to soften. Add 25 g ($\frac{1}{2}$ cup) of the mint, the vinegar and the remaining oil and stir until warmed through. In a large bowl, combine the pasta, chicken, spinach, onion mixture and remaining mint and toss well, seasoning to taste. Serve warm.

Serves 4

Vietnamese prawn salad

1 small Chinese cabbage, finely
  shredded
60 g (¼ cup) sugar
60 ml (¼ cup) fish sauce
80 ml (⅓ cup) lime juice
1 tablespoon white vinegar
1 small red onion, finely sliced
750 g (1 lb 10 oz) cooked tiger
  prawns (shrimp), peeled and
  deveined, tails intact
30 g (⅔ cup) chopped coriander
  (cilantro) leaves
30 g (⅔ cup) chopped Vietnamese
  mint leaves

Vietnamese mint leaves

Place the Chinese cabbage in a large
bowl, cover with plastic wrap and chill
for 30 minutes.

Put the sugar, fish sauce, lime juice,
vinegar and ½ teaspoon salt in a
small jug and mix well.

Toss together the shredded cabbage,
onion, prawns, coriander, mint and
dressing, and garnish with the extra
mint leaves.

Serves 6

Note: Vietnamese mint is available
from Asian grocery stores.

Scallops, ginger and spinach salad

300 g (10½ oz) scallops, without roe
100 g (2 cups) baby English spinach
 leaves
1 small red capsicum (pepper), cut
 into very fine strips
50 g (1¾ oz) bean sprouts
25 ml (1 fl oz) sake
1 tablespoon lime juice
2 teaspoons shaved palm sugar
 or soft brown sugar
1 teaspoon fish sauce

Remove any membrane or hard white muscle from the scallops. Lightly brush a chargrill pan or barbecue hotplate with oil. Cook the scallops in batches for 1 minute each side, or until cooked.

Divide the spinach, capsicum and bean sprouts among four plates. Arrange the scallops over the top.

To make the dressing, place the sake, lime juice, palm sugar and fish sauce in a small bowl, and mix together well. Pour over the salad and serve immediately.

Serves 4

Tuscan bread salad

200 g (7 oz) ciabatta bread
8 vine-ripened tomatoes
80 ml (1/3 cup) olive oil
1 tablespoon lemon juice
1 1/2 tablespoons red wine vinegar
6 anchovy fillets, finely chopped
1 tablespoon baby capers, rinsed,
   drained and finely chopped
1 garlic clove, crushed
30 g (1 cup) basil leaves

Preheat the oven to 220°C (425°F/ Gas 7). Tear the bread into 2 cm (3/4 inch) pieces, spread on a baking tray and bake for 5–7 minutes, or until golden on the outside. Leave the toasted bread on a cake rack to cool.

Score a cross in the base of each tomato. Place in a heatproof bowl and cover with boiling water. Leave for 30 seconds, then transfer to cold water and peel the skin away from the cross. Cut four of the tomatoes in half and squeeze the juice and seeds into a bowl, reserving and chopping the flesh. Add the oil, juice, vinegar, anchovies, capers and garlic to the tomato juice, and season.

Seed and slice the remaining tomatoes, and place in a large bowl with the reserved tomato and most of the basil. Add the dressing and toasted bread, and toss. Garnish with the remaining basil, season, and leave for at least 15 minutes. Serve at room temperature.

Serves 6

Spicy lamb and noodle salad

1 tablespoon five-spice powder
60 ml (1/4 cup) vegetable oil
2 garlic cloves, crushed
2 lamb backstraps or fillets (about
   250 g/9 oz each)
500 g (1 lb 2 oz) fresh Shanghai
   (wheat) noodles
1 1/2 teaspoons sesame oil
80 g (3 oz) snow pea (mangetout)
   sprouts
1/2 red capsicum (pepper), thinly sliced
4 spring onions (scallions), thinly
   sliced on the diagonal
2 tablespoons sesame seeds, toasted

Dressing
1 tablespoon finely chopped fresh
   ginger
1 tablespoon Chinese black vinegar
1 tablespoon Chinese rice wine
2 tablespoons peanut oil
2 teaspoons chilli oil

Combine the five-spice powder,
2 tablespoons of the vegetable oil
and garlic in a large bowl. Add the
lamb and turn to coat well. Cover
and marinate for 30 minutes.

Cook the noodles in a large saucepan
of boiling water for 4–5 minutes, or
until tender. Drain, rinse with cold
water and drain again. Add the
sesame oil and toss to combine.

Heat the remaining vegetable oil in
a large frying pan. Cook the lamb over
medium–high heat for 3 minutes each
side for medium–rare, or until cooked
to your liking. Rest for 5 minutes, then
thinly slice across the grain.

To make the dressing, combine the
ginger, Chinese black vinegar, rice
wine, peanut oil and chilli oil.

Place the noodles, lamb strips,
snowpea sprouts, capsicum, spring
onion and the dressing in a large bowl
and toss gently until well combined.
Sprinkle with the sesame seeds
and serve immediately.

Serves 4

Pasta salad with tomato and pesto

140 ml (5 fl oz) olive oil
500 g (1 lb 2 oz) cherry tomatoes
5 garlic cloves, unpeeled
400 g (14 oz) penne pasta
90 g (1/3 cup) pesto
3 tablespoons balsamic vinegar

basil leaves

Preheat the oven to 180°C (350°F/ Gas 4). Place 2 tablespoons of oil in a roasting dish and place in the hot oven for 5 minutes. Add the tomatoes and garlic to the dish, season well and toss until the tomatoes are well coated. Return to the oven and roast for 30 minutes.

Meanwhile, cook the pasta in a large saucepan of rapidly boiling water until *al dente*. Drain and transfer to a large serving bowl.

Squeeze the flesh from the roasted garlic cloves into a bowl. Add the remaining olive oil, the pesto, vinegar and 3 tablespoons of the tomato cooking juices. Season with a little salt and pepper, and toss to combine. Add to the pasta and mix well, ensuring that the pasta is coated in the dressing. Gently stir in the cherry tomatoes, then scatter with basil. This salad can be prepared up to 4 hours ahead, and served warm or cold.

Serves 4

Indian marinated chicken salad

60 ml (¼ cup) lemon juice
1½ teaspoons garam masala
1 teaspoon ground turmeric
1 tablespoon finely grated fresh
  ginger
2 garlic cloves, finely chopped
3½ tablespoons vegetable oil
3 chicken breast fillets (650 g/
  1 lb 7 oz)
1 onion, thinly sliced
2 zucchini (courgettes), thinly sliced
  on the diagonal
100 g (3½ oz) watercress leaves
150 g (5½ oz) freshly shelled peas
2 ripe tomatoes, finely chopped
30 g (1 cup) coriander (cilantro) leaves

Dressing
1 teaspoon cumin seeds
½ teaspoon coriander seeds
90 g (⅓ cup) natural yoghurt
2 tablespoons chopped mint
2 tablespoons lemon juice

Combine the lemon juice, garam masala, turmeric, ginger, garlic and 2 teaspoons oil in a large bowl. Add the chicken fillets and onion, toss to coat in the marinade, cover, and refrigerate for 1 hour.

Remove and discard the onion, then heat 2 tablespoons of oil in a large frying pan. Cook the chicken for about 4–5 minutes on each side, or until it is cooked through. Remove the chicken from the pan and leave for 5 minutes. Cut each breast across the grain into 1 cm (½ inch) slices.

Heat the remaining oil in the pan and cook the zucchini for 2 minutes, or until lightly golden and tender. Toss with the watercress in a large bowl. Cook the peas in boiling water for 5 minutes, or until tender, then drain. Rinse under cold water to cool. Add to the salad with the tomato, chicken and coriander.

For the dressing, gently roast the cumin and coriander seeds in a dry frying pan for 1–2 minutes, or until fragrant. Remove, then pound the seeds to a powder. Mix with the yoghurt, mint and lemon juice, then gently fold through the salad.

Serves 4

Greek peppered lamb salad

300 g (10½ oz) lamb backstraps
  or fillets
1½ tablespoons black pepper
3 vine-ripened tomatoes, cut into
  8 wedges
2 Lebanese (short) cucumbers, sliced
150 g (5½ oz) lemon and garlic
  marinated Kalamata olives, drained
  (reserving 1½ tablespoons oil)
100 g (3½ oz) Greek feta cheese,
  cubed
¾ teaspoon dried oregano
1 tablespoon lemon juice
1 tablespoon extra virgin olive oil

Roll the backstraps in the pepper, pressing the pepper on with your fingers. Cover and refrigerate for 15 minutes.

Place the tomato, cucumber, olives, feta and ½ teaspoon of the dried oregano in a bowl.

Heat a chargrill pan or barbecue hotplate, brush with oil and when very hot, cook the lamb for 2–3 minutes on each side, or until cooked to your liking. Keep warm.

Whisk together the lemon juice, extra virgin olive oil, reserved Kalamata oil and the remaining dried oregano. Season. Pour half the dressing over the salad, toss together and arrange on a serving platter.

Cut the lamb on the diagonal into 1 cm (½ inch) thick slices and arrange on top of the salad. Pour the remaining dressing on top and serve.

Serves 4

Chilli chicken and cashew salad

3 tablespoons sweet chilli sauce
2 tablespoons lime juice
2 teaspoons fish sauce
2 tablespoons chopped coriander
  (cilantro)
1 garlic clove, crushed
1 small red chilli, finely chopped
1½ teaspoons grated fresh ginger
2 tablespoons olive oil
600 g (1 lb 5 oz) chicken breast fillets
100 g (3½ oz) salad leaves
250 g (9 oz) cherry tomatoes, halved
100 g (3½ oz) Lebanese (short)
  cucumber, cut into bite-sized
  chunks
50 g (1¾ oz) snow pea (mangetout)
  sprouts, trimmed
80 g (½ cup) cashew nuts, roughly
  chopped

Combine the chilli sauce, lime juice, fish sauce, coriander, garlic, chilli, ginger and 1 tablespoon of the oil in a large bowl.

Heat the remaining oil in a frying pan or chargrill pan over medium heat until hot, and cook the chicken for 5–8 minutes on each side, or until cooked through. While still hot, slice each breast widthways into 1 cm (½ inch) slices and toss in the bowl with the dressing. Leave to cool slightly.

Combine the salad leaves, cherry tomatoes, cucumber chunks and snowpea sprouts in a serving bowl. Add the chicken and all of the dressing, and toss gently until the leaves are lightly coated. Scatter with chopped cashews and serve.

Serves 4

Warm pork salad with blue cheese croutons

125 ml (½ cup) olive oil
1 large garlic clove, crushed
400 g (14 oz) pork fillet, cut into
  5 mm (¼ inch) slices
1 small or ½ a large baguette, cut
  into 20 x 5 mm (¼ inch) slices
100 g (3½ oz) blue cheese, crumbled
2 tablespoons sherry vinegar
½ teaspoon soft brown sugar
150 g (5½ oz) mixed salad leaves

Place the olive oil and garlic in a jar and shake well. Heat 2 teaspoons of the garlic oil in a frying pan, add half the pork and cook for 1 minute on each side. Remove and keep warm. Add another 2 teaspoons garlic oil and cook the remaining pork. Remove. Season the pork with salt and black pepper to taste.

Lay the bread slices on a baking tray and brush with a little garlic oil on one side. Cook the bread under a hot griller (broiler) until golden. Turn the bread over, sprinkle with the crumbled blue cheese, then return to the griller and cook until the cheese has melted (this will happen very quickly).

Add the sherry vinegar and sugar to the remaining garlic oil and shake well. Place the salad leaves in a large bowl, add the pork and pour on the salad dressing. Toss well. Place a mound of salad in the middle of four serving plates and arrange five croutons around the edge of each salad. Serve the salad immediately.

Serves 4

Seafood salad

500 g (1 lb 2 oz) small squid
1 kg (2 lb 4 oz) large clams
1 kg (2 lb 4 oz) black mussels
500 g (1 lb 2 oz) raw medium prawns
  (shrimp), peeled, deveined,
  tails intact
5 tablespoons finely chopped flat-leaf
  (Italian) parsley

Dressing
2 tablespoons lemon juice
80 ml (1/3 cup) olive oil
1 garlic clove, crushed

Gently pull apart the body and
tentacles of the squid to separate.
Remove the head by cutting below
the eyes. Push out the beak and
discard. Pull the quill from the body
of the squid and discard. Under cold
running water, pull away all the skin
(the flaps can be used). Rinse well,
then slice the squid into rings.

Scrub the clams and mussels and
remove the beards. Discard any that
are cracked or don't close when
tapped. Rinse under running water.
Fill a saucepan with 2 cm (3/4 inches)
water, add the clams and mussels,
cover, and boil for 4–5 minutes,
or until the shells open. Remove,
reserving the liquid. Discard any that
do not open. Remove the mussels
and clams from their shells and place
in a bowl.

Bring 1 litre (4 cups) water to the boil
and add the prawns and squid. Cook
for 3–4 minutes, or until the prawns
turn pink and the squid is tender. Drain
and add to the clams and mussels.

To make the dressing, whisk all of the
ingredients together. Season. Pour
over the seafood, add 4 tablespoons
of the parsley and toss to coat. Cover
and refrigerate for 30–40 minutes.
Sprinkle with the remaining parsley
and serve with fresh bread.

Serves 4

Marinated grilled tofu salad with ginger miso dressing

80 ml (⅓ cup) tamari, shoyu or light
    soy sauce
2 teaspoons oil
2 garlic cloves, crushed
1 teaspoon grated fresh ginger
1 teaspoon chilli paste
500 g (1 lb 2 oz) firm tofu, cut into
    2 cm (¾ inch) cubes
400 g (14 oz) mixed salad leaves
1 Lebanese (short) cucumber, finely
    sliced
250 g (9 oz) cherry tomatoes, halved
2 teaspoons oil, extra

Dressing
2 teaspoons white miso paste
2 tablespoons mirin
1 teaspoon sesame oil
1 teaspoon grated fresh ginger
1 teaspoon finely chopped chives
1 tablespoon toasted sesame seeds

Mix together the tamari, oil, garlic, ginger, chilli paste and ½ teaspoon salt in a bowl. Add the tofu and mix until well coated. Marinate for at least 10 minutes, or preferably overnight. Drain and reserve the marinade.

To make the dressing, combine the miso with 125 ml (½ cup) hot water and leave until the miso dissolves. Add the mirin, sesame oil, ginger, chives and sesame seeds and stir thoroughly until it begins to thicken.

Combine the mixed salad leaves, cucumber and tomato in a serving bowl and leave until ready to serve.

Heat the extra oil in a chargrill pan or barbecue hotplate. Add the tofu and cook over medium heat for 4 minutes, or until golden brown. Pour on the reserved marinade and cook for 1 minute over high heat. Remove from the chargrill and allow to cool for 5 minutes.

Add the tofu to the salad, drizzle with the dressing and toss well.

Serves 4

Note: Miso is Japanese bean paste and plays an important part in their cuisine. It is commonly used in soups, dressings, on grilled (broiled) foods and as a flavouring for pickles.

Thai beef salad

500 g (1 lb 2 oz) rump steak
3½ tablespoons lime juice
2 tablespoons fish sauce
1 teaspoon grated palm sugar
2 garlic cloves, crushed
1 stem lemon grass, white part
  only, finely sliced
2 small fresh red chillies, finely sliced
4 red Asian shallots, finely sliced
15–20 fresh mint leaves
15 g (½ cup) fresh coriander
  (cilantro) leaves
125 g (4½ oz) cherry tomatoes,
  halved
1 Lebanese (short) cucumber, halved
  lengthwise and thinly sliced
180 g (3 cups) shredded Chinese
  cabbage
20 g (¼ cup) prepared Asian
  fried onions
1 tablespoon prepared Asian
  fried garlic
40 g (¼ cup) crushed peanuts,
  to garnish

Heat a non-stick frying pan over medium–high heat until very hot. Cook the steak for 4 minutes each side, then remove and cool.

Combine the lime juice, fish sauce, palm sugar, garlic, lemon grass and chilli and stir to dissolve the sugar. Add the shallots, mint and coriander. Thinly slice the beef across the grain, and toss through the mixture. Chill for 15 minutes. Add the tomato and cucumber and toss well. Arrange the cabbage on a serving platter and top with the beef mixture. Sprinkle with the fried onion, garlic and peanuts.

Serves 4

Roasted tomato and bocconcini salad

8 Roma (plum) tomatoes, halved
pinch of sugar
125 ml (½ cup) olive oil
15 g (¼ cup) torn basil
2 tablespoons balsamic vinegar
350 g (12 oz) cherry bocconcini or
  baby fresh mozzarella cheese
160 g (5¾ oz) mizuna lettuce

sea salt

Preheat the oven to 150°C (300°F/ Gas 2). Place the tomato, cut-side-up, on a rack over a baking tray lined with baking paper. Sprinkle with salt, cracked black pepper, and a pinch of sugar. Roast for 2 hours, then remove from the oven and allow to cool.

Combine the oil and basil in a saucepan, and stir gently over medium heat for 3–5 minutes, or until it is very hot, but not smoking. Remove from the heat and discard the basil. Mix 2 tablespoons of oil with the vinegar.

Toss together the tomato, bocconcini and lettuce. Arrange the salad in a shallow serving bowl and drizzle with the dressing. Sprinkle with sea salt and cracked black pepper.

Serves 6

Notes: If cherry bocconcini are unavailable, use regular bocconcini cut into quarters.
Leftover basil oil can be stored in a clean jar in the refrigerator, and is great in pasta sauces.

Lamb, capsicum and cucumber salad

1 red onion, very thinly sliced
1 red capsicum (pepper), very thinly
  sliced
1 green capsicum (pepper), very thinly
  sliced
2 large Lebanese (short) cucumbers,
  cut into batons
20 g (1/3 cup) shredded mint
3 tablespoons chopped dill
60 ml (1/4 cup) olive oil
600 g (1 lb 5 oz) lamb backstraps or
  fillets
80 ml (1/3 cup) lemon juice
2 small garlic cloves, crushed
100 ml (3 1/2 fl oz) extra virgin olive oil

Combine the onion, red and green
capsicum, cucumber, mint and dill
in a large bowl.

Heat a chargrill pan or frying pan until
hot. Drizzle with the oil and cook the
lamb for 2–3 minutes on each side,
or until it is tender but still a little pink.
Remove from the pan and allow to
rest for 5 minutes. Thinly slice the
lamb and add to the salad, tossing
to mix.

Combine the lemon juice and garlic
in a small jug, then whisk in the extra
virgin olive oil with a fork until well
combined. Season with salt and black
pepper, then gently toss the dressing
through the salad.

Serves 4

Note: This salad is delicious served
on fresh or toasted Turkish bread
spread with hummus.

Smoked trout Caesar salad

350 g (12 oz) skinless smoked trout
fillets
300 g (10½ oz) green beans, halved
6 tinned artichokes, drained, rinsed
and quartered
2 eggs
1 small garlic clove, chopped
2 teaspoons Dijon mustard
2 tablespoons white wine vinegar
80 ml (⅓ cup) olive oil
6 slices (200 g/7 oz) day-old Italian-
style bread (ciabatta), cut into
2 cm (¾ inch) cubes
2 tablespoons capers, drained
1 baby cos (romaine) lettuce, leaves
separated
40 g (½ cup) freshly shaved
Parmesan cheese

Flake the trout into 4 cm (1½ inch) shards and place in a bowl. Cook the beans in boiling water for 3 minutes, or until tender and still bright green. Refresh under cold water. Add to the bowl, with the artichoke.

Poach the eggs in simmering water for 40 seconds, or until just cooked. Place in a food processor with the garlic, mustard and vinegar, and process until smooth. With the motor running, add 2 tablespoons oil in a thin stream, processing until thick and creamy. Season to taste.

Heat the remaining oil in a frying pan, add the bread and capers, and cook over high heat for 3–5 minutes, or until golden. Line four bowls with the cos leaves. Divide the trout mixture among the bowls, drizzle with the dressing and top with the croutons, capers and Parmesan.

Serves 4

Chargrilled baby octopus salad

1 kg (2 lb 4 oz) baby octopus
1 teaspoon sesame oil
2 tablespoons lime juice
2 tablespoons fish sauce
60 ml (¼ cup) sweet chilli sauce
200 g (7 oz) mixed salad leaves
1 red capsicum (pepper), very thinly
  sliced
2 small Lebanese (short) cucumbers,
  seeded and cut into ribbons
4 red Asian shallots, chopped
100 g (3½ oz) toasted unsalted
  peanuts, chopped

To clean the octopus, remove the head from the tentacles by cutting just underneath the eyes. To clean the head, carefully slit the head open and remove the gut. Cut it in half. Push out the beak from the centre of the tentacles, then cut the tentacles into sets of four or two, depending on their size. Pull the skin away from the head and tentacles if it comes away easily. The eyes will come off as you pull off the skin.

To make the marinade, combine the sesame oil, lime juice, fish sauce and chilli sauce in a shallow, non-metallic bowl. Add the octopus, and stir to coat. Cover and chill for 2 hours.

Heat a chargrill pan or barbecue hotplate to hot. Drain the octopus, reserving the marinade, then cook in batches for 3–5 minutes, turning occasionally.

Pour the reserved marinade into a small saucepan, bring to the boil and cook for 2 minutes, or until it has slightly thickened.

Divide the salad leaves among four plates, scatter with capsicum and cucumber, then top with the octopus. Drizzle with the marinade and top with the Asian shallots and peanuts.

Serves 3–4

Italian tomato salad

6 Roma (plum) tomatoes
2 teaspoons capers, rinsed
   and drained
6 basil leaves, torn
1 tablespoon olive oil
1 tablespoon balsamic vinegar
2 garlic cloves, crushed
½ teaspoon honey

Cut the tomatoes lengthways into quarters. Place on a grill tray, skin-side-down, and cook under a hot griller (broiler) for 4–5 minutes, or until golden. Cool to room temperature and place in a bowl.

Combine the capers, basil leaves, olive oil, balsamic vinegar, crushed garlic and honey in a bowl, season with salt and freshly ground black pepper, and pour over the tomatoes. Toss gently.

Serves 6

Tuna and white bean salad

400 g (14 oz) tuna steaks
1 small red onion, thinly sliced
1 tomato, seeded and chopped
1 small red capsicum (pepper), thinly
  sliced
2 x 400 g (14 oz) tins cannellini beans
2 garlic cloves, crushed
1 teaspoon chopped thyme
4 tablespoons finely chopped flat-leaf
  (Italian) parsley
1 1/2 tablespoons lemon juice
80 ml (1/3 cup) extra virgin olive oil
1 teaspoon honey
olive oil, for brushing
100 g (3 1/2 oz) rocket (arugula)
1 teaspoon lemon zest

Place the tuna steaks on a plate, sprinkle with cracked black pepper on both sides, cover with plastic wrap and refrigerate until needed.

Combine the onion, tomato and capsicum in a large bowl. Rinse the cannellini beans under cold running water for 30 seconds, drain and add to the bowl with the garlic, thyme and 3 tablespoons of the parsley.

Place the lemon juice, oil and honey in a small saucepan, bring to the boil, then simmer, stirring, for 1 minute, or until the honey dissolves. Remove from the heat.

Brush a chargrill pan or barbecue hotplate with olive oil, and heat until very hot. Cook the tuna for 1 minute on each side. The meat should still be pink in the middle. Slice into 3 cm (1 1/4 inch) cubes and combine with the salad. Pour on the warm dressing and toss well.

Place the rocket on a platter. Top with the salad, season and garnish with the zest and remaining parsley.

Serves 4–6

Soba noodle salad
with tahini dressing

200 g (7 oz) snake beans or green
  beans
200 g (7 oz) soba noodles
1 tablespoon tahini
1 small garlic clove, crushed
1 1/2 tablespoons rice vinegar
1 1/2 tablespoons olive oil
1/2 teaspoon sesame oil
1 teaspoon soy sauce
2 teaspoons sugar
2 spring onions (scallions), finely
  sliced
3 teaspoons black sesame seeds

Trim the beans, and cut into long strips on the diagonal. Place in a saucepan of boiling water and return to the boil for 2 minutes, or until tender. Drain and refresh under cold running water. Drain.

Cook the noodles in boiling water for 3–4 minutes, or until they are tender. Drain and refresh under cold water, then drain again.

Combine the tahini, crushed garlic, rice vinegar, olive oil, sesame oil, soy sauce, sugar and 2 teaspoons warm water in a screw-top jar. Shake well and season to taste.

Combine the beans, noodles, spring onion and sesame seeds in a serving bowl, add the dressing and toss lightly to combine. Serve immediately.

Serves 4–6

Note: Add the dressing as close to serving as possible, as it will be absorbed by the noodles.

Fresh beetroot and goat's cheese salad

1 kg (2 lb 4 oz) (4 bulbs with leaves) fresh beetroot
200 g (7 oz) green beans
1 tablespoon red wine vinegar
2 tablespoons extra virgin olive oil
1 garlic clove, crushed
1 tablespoon capers in brine, rinsed, drained and coarsely chopped
100 g (3½ oz) goat's cheese

Trim the leaves from the beetroot. Scrub the bulbs and wash the leaves well. Bring a large saucepan of water to the boil, add the beetroot, then reduce the heat and simmer, covered, for 30 minutes, or until tender when pierced with the point of a knife. (The cooking time may vary depending on the size of the bulbs.) Drain and cool. Peel the skins off the beetroot and cut the bulbs into wedges.

Meanwhile, bring a saucepan of water to the boil, add the beans and cook for 3 minutes, or until just tender. Remove with tongs and plunge into a bowl of cold water. Drain well. Add the beetroot leaves to the boiling water and cook for 3–5 minutes, or until the leaves and stems are tender. Drain, plunge into a bowl of cold water, then drain well again.

To make the dressing, put the vinegar, oil, garlic, capers, ½ teaspoon salt and ½ teaspoon cracked black pepper in a jar and shake well. Divide the beans and beetroot wedges and leaves among four plates. Crumble the goat's cheese over the top and drizzle with the dressing.

Serves 4

Beef satay salad

2 teaspoons tamarind pulp
½ teaspoon sesame oil
2 tablespoons soy sauce
2 teaspoons soft brown sugar
2 garlic cloves, crushed
1 tablespoon lime juice
700 g (1 lb 9 oz) rump steak
1 tablespoon peanut oil
6 large cos (romaine) lettuce leaves,
  washed, dried and shredded
1 red capsicum (pepper), julienned
180 g (2 cups) bean sprouts
2 tablespoons fried onion flakes

Satay sauce
2 red chillies, chopped
½ teaspoon shrimp paste
1 garlic clove
6 red Asian shallots
2 teaspoons peanut oil
250 ml (1 cup) coconut milk
1 tablespoon lime juice
120 g (¾ cup) unsalted roasted
  peanuts, finely ground in a food
  processor
1 tablespoon kecap manis
1 tablespoon soft brown sugar
1 tablespoon fish sauce
2 makrut (kaffir) lime leaves, shredded

Combine the tamarind pulp and 60 ml (¼ cup) of boiling water and allow to cool. Mash the pulp with your fingertips to dissolve it, then strain, reserving the liquid. Discard the pulp.

Put the sesame oil, soy sauce, sugar, garlic, lime juice and 2 tablespoons of tamarind water in a large bowl. Add the steak, turn to coat, and cover with plastic wrap. Chill for 2 hours.

Meanwhile, to make the satay sauce, process the chillies, shrimp paste, garlic and shallots to a paste in a food processor. Heat the oil in a frying pan and cook the paste for 3 minutes. Add the coconut milk, lime juice, ground peanuts, remaining tamarind water, kecap manis, sugar, fish sauce and makrut lime leaves. Cook over medium heat until thickened. Thin with 125 ml (½ cup) water, and return to the boil for 2 minutes. Season.

Heat the peanut oil in a frying pan over high heat, and cook the steak for 3 minutes on each side, or until medium–rare. Leave for 3 minutes, then thinly slice. Toss the steak slices in a large bowl with the lettuce, capsicum and bean sprouts. Pile onto serving plates, drizzle with the satay sauce, and sprinkle with the fried onion flakes.

Serves 4

Modern salad Niçoise

60 ml (¼ cup) lemon juice
1 garlic clove, crushed
140 ml (5 fl oz) olive oil
400 g (14 oz) waxy potatoes, such as
  Charlotte or Kipfler
3 eggs
120 g (4½ oz) green beans, trimmed
1 green capsicum (pepper), seeded
  and sliced
120 g (4½ oz) black olives
300 g (10½ oz) firm, ripe tomatoes,
  cut into wedges
100 g (3½ oz) cucumber, cut into
  chunks
3 spring onions (scallions), cut into
  2 cm (¾ inch) pieces
600 g (1 lb 5 oz) fresh tuna steaks

Place the lemon juice, garlic and
120 ml (4 fl oz) of olive oil in a jar with
a screw-top lid. Season and shake
the jar well to combine.

Boil the potatoes in a saucepan of
salted water for 10–12 minutes, or
until tender. Add the eggs for the final
8 minutes of cooking. Drain, cool the
eggs under cold water, then peel and
quarter. Cool the potatoes, then cut
into chunks. Bring a saucepan of
salted water to the boil, add the green
beans and blanch for 3 minutes. Drain
and refresh under cold water. Drain
well, then slice in half on the diagonal.

Place the potato and beans in a large
bowl, and add the capsicum, olives,
tomatoes, cucumber and spring
onion. Strain the garlic from the
dressing, then shake again so it is
combined. Pour half over the salad,
toss and transfer to a serving dish.

Heat a frying pan over very high heat.
Add the remaining olive oil and allow
to heat. Season the tuna steaks well
on both sides and cook for 2 minutes
on each side, or until rare. Allow the
tuna to cool for 5 minutes, then slice
thinly. Arrange on top of the salad
with the eggs, and drizzle with the
remaining dressing.

Serves 4

Chargrilled chicken and pasta salad

375 g (13 oz) penne
100 ml (3½ fl oz) olive oil
4 long, thin eggplants (aubergines),
   thinly sliced on the diagonal
2 chicken breast fillets
2 teaspoons lemon juice
15 g (½ cup) chopped flat-leaf (Italian)
   parsley
270 g (9¾ oz) chargrilled red
   capsicum (pepper), drained
   and sliced (see Note)
155 g (5½ oz) fresh asparagus
   spears, trimmed, blanched and
   cut into 5 cm (2 inch) lengths
85 g (3 oz) semi-dried (sun-blushed)
   tomatoes, finely sliced

grated Parmesan cheese, optional

Cook the pasta in a large saucepan of boiling water until *al dente*. Drain, return to the pan and keep warm. Heat 2 tablespoons of the oil in a large frying pan over high heat and cook the eggplant for 4–5 minutes, or until golden and cooked through.

Heat a lightly oiled chargrill pan or barbecue hotplate over high heat and cook the chicken for 5 minutes each side, or until browned and cooked through. Cut into thick slices. Combine the lemon juice, parsley and the remaining oil in a small jar and shake well. Return the pasta to the heat, toss through the dressing, chicken, eggplant, capsicum, asparagus and tomato until well mixed and warmed through. Season with black pepper. Serve warm with a scattering of grated Parmesan, if desired.

Serves 4

Note: Jars of chargrilled capsicum can be bought at the supermarket; otherwise, visit your local deli.

Prawn and fennel salad

1.25 kg (2 lb 12 oz) raw large prawns
  (shrimp), peeled and deveined
1 large fennel bulb (400 g/14 oz),
  thinly sliced
300 g (10½ oz) watercress
2 tablespoons finely chopped chives
125 ml (½ cup) extra virgin olive oil
60 ml (¼ cup) lemon juice
1 tablespoon Dijon mustard
1 large garlic clove, finely chopped

Bring a saucepan of water to the boil, then add the prawns, return to the boil and simmer for 2 minutes, or until the prawns turn pink and are cooked through. Drain and leave to cool. Pat the prawns dry with paper towels and slice in half lengthways. Place in a large serving bowl.

Add the fennel, watercress and chives to the bowl and mix well.

To make the dressing, whisk the oil, lemon juice, mustard and garlic together until combined. Pour the dressing over the salad, season with salt and cracked black pepper and toss gently. Arrange the salad on serving plates and serve immediately.

Serves 4